MONTICELLO PUBLIC LIBRARY
512 E. LAKE AVE.
MONTICELLO, WI 53570

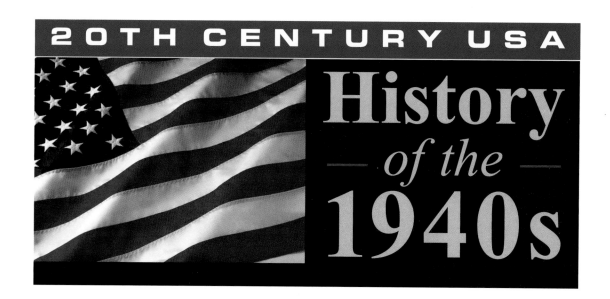

20TH CENTURY USA

History of the 1940s

Rennay Craats

MONTICELLO PUBLIC LIBRARY
512 E. LAKE AVE.
MONTICELLO, WI 53570

WEIGL PUBLISHERS INC.

Published by Weigl Publishers Inc.
123 South Broad Street, Box 227
Mankato, MN, USA 56002
Web site: http://www.weigl.com

Copyright © 2002 WEIGL PUBLISHERS INC.
All rights reserved. No part of this publication may be reproduced, stored in
a retrieval system, or transmitted in any form or by any means, electronic,
mechanical, photocopying, recording, or otherwise, without the prior written
permission of Weigl Publishers Inc.

Library of Congress Cataloging-in-Publication Data available upon request
from the publisher. Fax (507) 388-2746 for the attention of the Publishing
Records Department.

ISBN 1-930954-19-0

Printed and bound in the United States of America
1 2 3 4 5 6 7 8 9 0   05 04 03 02 01

Senior Editor
Jared Keen

Series Editor
Carlotta Lemieux

Copy Editor
Heather Kissock

Layout and Design
Warren Clark
Carla Pelky

Photo Research
Joe Nelson

Photograph Credits

American Stock/Archive Photos: pages 22, 37; Archive Photos: pages 3B, 16, 21, 23T, 24, 25T, 25B, 26, 27, 31, 42; Bettmann/CORBIS: pages 6BL, 9, 20, 23B, 28T, 29, 34; CORBIS: pages 14, 38; Hulton Ghetty/Archive Photos: pages 33B, 35; Moore Memorial Library Texas City: page 8; National Archives of Canada: pages 3BR, 15, 32, 33T, 43; Photodisc: pages 3MR, 36; Photofest: pages 3T, 10, 11, 12T, 12B, 13, 40, 41; Photo File/Archive Photos: page 31T; Popperfoto/Archive Photos: pages 7BR, 18, 19T, 30B; Peter Ruhe/Archive Photos: page 19B; Sporting News/Archive Photos: page 28B; Jeff Stern/Archive Photos: page 7BL, 17.

Every reasonable effort has been made to trace ownership and to obtain permission to reprint copyright material. The publishers would be pleased to have any errors or omissions brought to their attention so that they may be corrected in subsequent printings.

Contents

Entertainment 10

Literature 24

Fashion 36

MONTICELLO PUBLIC LIBRARY
512 E. LAKE AVE.
MONTICELLO, WI 53570

3/12/02 Davidson 17⁵⁵

Introduction

Girls of Summer

Jackie Robinson Triumphs

Truman's Fair Deal

BRACEROS

Vinyl Records Arrive

Harbor Disaster

Bugs Bunny

Joe Louis Champ

Sound Barrier Broken

Gandhi Calms Riots

The 1940s began with the world at war. At first, few Americans thought they should become involved. That all changed in 1941 when Japan attacked Pearl Harbor. U.S. troops went to war, and Americans at home did all they could to support them. This included anything from donating scrap metal for weapons to rationing supplies. Women marched into factories to fill jobs left by **enlisted** men. Other women joined the military to perform administrative tasks, freeing men for active duty.

Entertainment changed with the war, too. Hollywood brought the battlefield home through films. Some stars performed at military bases, while others posed for pin-up photographs. Musicians such as the Andrews Sisters and Glenn Miller kept spirits up on army bases. In sports, Joe DiMaggio and Ted Williams wowed baseball fans with their amazing skills and hitting streaks, until they, too

World at War

Woman Power

Israel Independent

Holocaust

Native Son

Dance the Jitterbug

Atomic Bomb

Transistor Radio Here

Free Nylons

joined the armed forces and went off to war. Fans turned their cheers to the new All American Girls' Professional Baseball League. These talented women athletes gave fans their money's worth and filled the void in baseball. Everything, from fashion to immigration, was affected by World War II.

The forties was a decade of tears and hardship as well as one of joy and excitement. *20th Century USA: History of the 1940s* brings some of the important events and people to light. These are only a few of many stories that unfolded during the forties. You can discover more exciting history at your library through microfilm copies of old newspapers and magazines. The Internet, encyclopedias, and reference books are also great places to learn more about the forties. For now, turn the page and travel back in time to the 1940s.

1940

Bugs, Elmer, and Daffy take the entertainment scene by storm. Warner Brothers' animated heroes are a hit. Page 11 has more about the cartoon sensation.

1940

Franklin Roosevelt does what no other president has done before. Find out more on page 20.

1940

American scientists celebrate a discovery. Plutonium is the newest element. See how dangerous this discovery could be on page 26.

1941

African Americans take up the fight for their rights. Learn about their argument and discover what happened on page 20.

1941

With the bombing of Pearl Harbor, the U.S. enters World War II. Learn more about this on page 21.

1942

Humphrey Bogart and Ingrid Bergman have Americans playing it again and again. Page 12 has the scoop on a Hollywood film classic.

1942

Adolf Hitler's Nazis meet to decide how to eliminate Jewish people. The result was the Holocaust. Learn more on page 17.

1942

After Pearl Harbor, many Americans mistrusted Japanese people. Fear and hatred led to Japanese-American **internment** during the war. Hundreds of thousands are moved inland to camps. Find out more on page 33.

1942

A football celebration turns into a nightmare in Boston. Find out what happened at the Cocoanut Grove on page 9.

1943

The Magnuson Act alters U.S. policies on immigration. Read about its effects on page 39.

1943

Times are tough in the U.S. The standard of living is not what it was just a few years before. Turn to page 34 to find out about the nation's economic troubles.

1944

Allied troops reclaim Europe. This is a major victory. Turn to page 16 to find out more about **D-Day**.

1944

Women further the war effort. By this time, about 3.5 million women are working on assembly lines. Find out more about woman power on page 32.

1944

The world does not want a repeat of World War II. Leaders get together to make sure it can never happen again. After six weeks, an organization is established to help resolve conflict before it explodes into war. Page 43 has more about the United Nations.

African Americans

Women working

1945

President Roosevelt is dead. Harry Truman takes the helm. Read more about his entry into office on page 22.

1945

The Allies warn Japan to surrender. Japan refuses, so a U.S. bomber drops the first of two atomic bombs. Page 17 has details about the devastation and the end of the war.

1946

Nazi war criminals are brought to justice. Many are sentenced to death or life in prison for their role in this horrible war. Find out more about the Nuremburg trials on page 18.

1946

Scientists make ENIAC, the first computer of its kind. Find out about ENIAC's enormous size and speed on page 27.

1946

Women bare all, or almost all, on European beaches. The fad soon hits the U.S. Turn to page 15 to learn more about fashion that turned heads.

1947

A fighter pilot flies faster than anyone else has ever flown. He reaches speeds of **Mach** 1.06. Find out what this means on page 26.

1947

An explosion in Texas City triggers a disaster. Turn to page 8 to find out how a fire aboard the *Grandcamp* was responsible for hundreds of deaths.

1947

Jackie Robinson makes baseball history. He breaks the color barrier and becomes a Dodger. Find out more about this trailblazer on page 31.

1948

The Olympic Games are held again after World War II. American athletes prove that they are glad to be there. Find out how on page 29.

1948

Music lovers rejoice! New records mean they can listen to their favorite bands at home without changing the record every few minutes. Read more about LPs on page 14.

1948

The man who brought change through peaceful resistance is murdered. The world mourns the loss of a great man. Find out who he was on page 19.

1949

The world is told about an eerie future. Turn to page 25 to read more about Big Brother.

1949

After eleven years as champion, Joe Louis retires from boxing. Read about his amazing accomplishments on page 30.

1949

Twelve nations sign the North Atlantic Treaty. Learn about this important alliance on page 42.

Atomic bomb

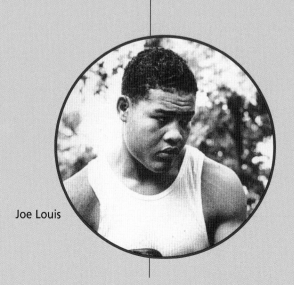

Joe Louis

Harbor Disaster

On April 15, 1947, a French freighter, the *Grandcamp*, arrived in Texas City. It was carrying peanuts, cotton, machinery, and twine and had docked to pick up 1,400 tons of ammonium nitrate fertilizer. That night, a fire started aboard the ship. The ship's officers did not try very hard to put the fire out, fearing that water would damage the rest of the cargo. By morning, thick smoke was billowing from the *Grandcamp*. The fire department ordered the ship to be towed out of the harbor—it was docked only 700 feet from the Monsanto chemical plant. The order came too late, and the ship exploded.

■ Smoke from the *Grandcamp* explosion filled the Texas City air.

The rumbling was felt 150 miles away and registered on a **seismograph** in Colorado.

That explosion set off another one—the chemical plant blew up moments later. Many people who had survived the first explosion were killed by the second one. Most of the business district was destroyed. Fires swept through Texas City, and rescue workers from neighboring cities flocked to the area to help. Early in the morning on April 17, another freighter loaded with nitrates exploded. The third blast was too much for people in Texas City. Many left, letting the new fires burn themselves out. About 468 people were said to have been killed, but the number was likely closer to 1,000 because of the uncertainty over the number of migrant dock workers.

HAWAI'IAN TSUNAMI

■ On April 1, 1946, an earthquake shook the Aleutian Trench in the north Pacific Ocean. Within minutes, a 100-foot wave created by the tremor crashed over Alaska's Scotch Cap lighthouse 70 miles away. Five people were killed, and the structure was ruined. The **tsunami** hit the California coast and five hours later approached the Hawai'ian Islands. There was no warning. Wave after wave, each about 50 feet high, crashed into Hawai'i. The city of Hilo was badly damaged. More than 1,000 buildings were destroyed or harmed, causing about $25 million in damages. In the end, 173 people were killed, and 163 were injured. The tsunami that rocked Hawai'i was the worst natural disaster in the island's history.

Empire State Building Collision

Colonel William Smith took off in his B-25 light bomber early in the morning of Saturday, July 28, 1945. He was flying from Bedford, Massachusetts, to Newark, New Jersey. As Smith neared his destination, he asked the tower at LaGuardia airfield for conditions. He was told that there was terrible visibility. A few minutes later, Smith's bomber broke through the cloudy skies over Manhattan and hit the tallest building in the world at the time.

Smith had crashed into the seventy-eighth and seventy-ninth floors of the Empire State Building. One of the bomber's engines tore away from the plane, skidded across a floor, crashed through walls, and flew out the other side of the building. Another engine hit the elevator shaft. The car plummeted down eighty floors. Roofs were set on fire by burning fuel. The crash caused severe damage. Thirteen people, including those in the plane, died, but this number could have been much higher—on a normal workday, 50,000 people would have been in the building.

■ Fire ripped through the Cocoanut Grove, claiming hundreds of lives.

Boston Fire

On November 28, 1942, a huge party was planned at Cocoanut Grove to celebrate the Boston College Boosters Club's victory over Holy Cross in the annual football game. In an upset, Holy Cross won, and the party was cancelled. Nearly 1,000 people went to the Cocoanut Grove anyway. That was twice as many people as the club was meant to hold. At about 10:00 PM, a busboy tried to replace a burned-out light bulb in the lounge. The room was dark, so he struck a match to see where the socket was—and he accidentally set a fake palm tree on fire. A bartender beat the flames with a wet rag, and another employee tried to find a fire extinguisher. Then, suddenly, flames leapt across the cloth ceiling and throughout the club. People scrambled to get out of the building. Many of the doors were locked, and the revolving door at the front was quickly jammed with people. The only other door that was unlocked opened inward. The rush of people pushing against the door made it difficult to open. Firefighters who hurried to the club could not get in through the body-blocked doors. Some people found a route through the basement to the street. Others jumped from a second-story window. Four hundred ninety-one people died in the fire.

Head-On Disaster

In December 1943, many rail passengers were eager to get home for the holidays. The Atlantic Coast Line ran trains north and south between Washington, D.C., and Florida almost daily. On December 16, sleet caused the Florida-bound train to derail near Lumberton, North Carolina. Its back three cars blocked the northbound track. As rail workers tried to get the train on track, they set up flares behind them to warn approaching trains. No one thought to set up warning flares on the northbound track. Twenty-five minutes later, the northbound train came speeding down the rails at 90 miles per hour. It crashed into the cars across the track. The impact destroyed the northbound train's locomotive and first eight cars. Some of the passengers who were in the southbound cars had climbed out earlier, but most had stayed inside because of the cold weather. Seventy-three people died, and 200 were injured. Most of the victims were servicemen on Christmas leave.

Hollywood Goes to War

During World War II, show-business stars donned army fatigues and performed for the troops overseas. Such stars as Bob Hope, the Andrews Sisters, Bing Crosby, Mickey Rooney, Al Jolson, George Burns, and Gracie Allen tried to boost **morale** with laughter and songs. Clark Gable, Jimmy Stewart, and other actors also performed for the troops, and Groucho Marx, James Cagney, and Judy Garland sold war bonds. Meanwhile, Hollywood also tried to keep up morale at home by making movies about the war. Directors such as John Huston and William Wyler created documentaries, while Walt Disney and B-movie star Ronald Reagan produced training films. More than 29,000 Hollywood celebrities served in the Armed Forces.

War movies such as *Purple Heart* boosted morale on the home front.

War Films

By 1942, Hollywood was scrambling to produce movies about the war. The heroes were "brave" U.S. soldiers, and the villains were often "evil" Germans or "cagey" Japanese.

Above Suspicion stars honeymooners Joan Crawford and Fred MacMurray, who are asked by the British to smuggle Nazi plans.

Purple Heart follows the war-crimes trial of a U.S. bomber crew captured by the Japanese. If the Americans reveal their base, the court will be lenient. The soldiers refuse to betray their country and are sentenced to death.

Other movies, including *Keep Your Powder Dry*, are comedies with a message. Lana Turner stars as a rich girl who joins the Women's Army Corps to prove that she deserves a huge inheritance. The film provides laughs, but in the end, Turner's character realizes how rewarding it is to serve her country. Hollywood kept pumping out war movies throughout the decade.

PIN-UPS GET SOLDIERS THROUGH WAR

Many female Hollywood stars did their part for the war effort by posing for photos to please the troops. These posters were plastered in barracks and footlockers across the war zone. Betty Grable showed off her legs while posing in a bathing suit. Grable's legs were so valuable that her movie studio insured them for $1 million. Rita Hayworth's stunning looks made her another **GI** favorite. Images of her in a nightgown were instant pleasers. These pictures caused a stir—many Americans insisted that they were too sexy. *Esquire* magazine included different pin-ups every month. In 1944, Postmaster General Frank Walker decided to put a stop to this. He announced that *Esquire* was banned from the mail. Soldiers were furious.

> "This is your war...You wanted it...You started it! And now you're going to get it, and it won't be finished until your dirty little empire is wiped off the face of the Earth!"
>
> From *Purple Heart*

Picture Perfect

Norman Rockwell, painter and illustrator, drew everyday events and people in America. Much of his work in the forties was patriotic and in support of the war. His illustrations often appeared on the covers of such popular magazines as *Ladies' Home Journal* and *Look*. They also graced the cover of the *Saturday Evening Post* for more than forty years. Rockwell paid close attention to detail, and his drawings often looked almost like photographs. They had an innocent and humorous emotion to them. During World War II, Rockwell created a young man who went off to fight in the war. On the cover of the *Post*, Americans followed this war "hero"—a character called Willie Gillis—and his family and friends. Parents loved Gillis—he reminded them of their own boys who had gone off to war. Gillis appeared on eleven *Saturday Evening Post* covers. Jug-eared Gillis was based on Rockwell's neighbor, Bob Buck, who posed for the illustrator before going to war himself. Like Gillis, Buck returned home safely. Rockwell's happy-ending illustrations gave Americans a smile every month and helped families through rough times.

Animated Heroes

In 1940, Warner Brothers introduced animated characters to U.S. television viewers. The lovable cartoons were welcomed instantly. Elmer Fudd hunted Bugs Bunny, who asked, "What's up, Doc?" Together with Daffy Duck, Porky Pig, Sylvester, and Road Runner, Bugs and Elmer appeared in six-

■ Bugs Bunny's arrival in Hollywood marked a shift to a new style of cartoon entertainment.

minute-long cartoons that challenged Disney's hold on animation. Warner Brothers artists wowed audiences with speed, unusual perspectives, and quick transformations—Bugs could turn into Carmen Miranda or spin his ears to take flight. Unlike the soft, safe humor of Disney productions, Warner Brothers films had a New York edge to them. Children and adults alike could not get enough of the new cartoons.

■ Humphrey Bogart's performance in *Casablanca* rocketed him to fame.

Casablanca a Classic

In 1942, the big screen was filled with war movies. None was as successful as *Casablanca*. In it, Rick, played by Humphrey Bogart, owns a restaurant in Morocco, where secret agents and military men meet. Rick's old flame Ilsa, played by Ingrid Bergman, walks into the restaurant. She stirs up memories and old feelings at a time of danger. *Casablanca*'s balance of romance, spies, and heartbreak is fueled with emotion. Audiences wept as Ilsa finally boarded the plane that took her to safety but away from Rick. The film was a hit, winning three Academy Awards for Best Picture, Best Director, and Best Screenplay.

FORTIES FALCON

■ In 1941, Americans rushed to theaters to watch Humphrey Bogart and Mary Astor on the big screen in *The Maltese Falcon*. The film is the story of private detective Sam Spade who is hired by Brigid O'Shaughnessy, played by Astor, to find her sister. In the process, Spade's partner is murdered, and Spade becomes involved in the search for a priceless antique. Over the course of his investigation, Spade finds out that his client is not who she says she is. She is one of the many people who want to get their hands on the valuable statuette. There were two other film versions of Dashiell Hammett's 1930 novel during the thirties, but the 1941 version became a classic.

The Duke

It was not long before an American actor became a symbol of the entire U.S. With his guns drawn at saloon doors, John Wayne became a Hollywood legend. He made more than 250 movies in his career, from *The Drop Kick* (1927) to *The Shootist* (1976). About ninety of these films were westerns, the kind of movie for which Wayne became famous. In 1939, Wayne was cast in the lead role in *Stagecoach*. He became an instant leading man, often playing the tough cowboy or the **invincible** soldier. Wayne's talent and special walk brought him attention and fame, along with an Academy Award in 1969 for *True Grit*. Besides acting, Wayne also directed and produced films.

■ John Wayne's all-American style helped make him a silver-screen hero.

"Who's on First?"

Bud Abbott and Lou Costello were comedy favorites. Their hilarious antics appeared on stage, radio, and television.

The funnymen got together by accident. Costello was performing in New York and asked Abbott, a ticket taker at the theater, to fill in for his sick straight man. The duo was a hit. They performed on Broadway and radio shows through the 1930s. Their most famous routine was a 1945 baseball skit called "Who's on First?" This comedy of errors centers around the strange names of the St. Louis Wolves baseball team. "Who" plays first, "What" plays second, and "I Don't Know" plays third. The confusion results in a routine that made the duo comedy legends.

■ America loved the comedic styles of Abbott and Costello.

Americans Tune In

Television was available in the 1930s in Europe, and in 1939, private U.S. stations experimented with it. RCA made radio and television sets and owned the National Broadcasting Company (NBC). This company sent live broadcasts from the New York World's Fair to viewers across the country. It also aired the first commercial, featuring a sportscaster selling soap and Wheaties cereal. Then, in 1940, the Federal Communications Commission delayed broadcasting until all companies involved could agree on the specifications of the new medium. This being done, on July 1, 1941, Americans could tune in to fifteen hours per week of regular television programming of sports, news, and cartoons. These programs were broadcast from New York.

All is Well with Welles

Orson Welles was fairly new to film when RKO movie studios offered him a contract with incredible freedom. He accepted, and the result was *Citizen Kane*. Welles broke the rules with this film. He presented audiences with a broken story line, great time lapses between scenes, unusual camera angles, and action happening in the background as well as in the foreground. Welles starred in, co-wrote, and directed the 1941 film about a corrupt newspaper tycoon. The character was modeled on the powerful newspaper owner William Randolph Hearst, who tried to get the film destroyed. Hearst threatened to publish **exposés**, MGM studios offered to buy the film so they could destroy it, and many theaters would not show the movie. But RKO would not back down. The movie drew rave reviews, with the *New York Times* reviewer saying that *Citizen Kane* was "close to being the most sensational film ever made in Hollywood." At first, the movie lost money, but since its opening it has become one of the most influential films in movie history.

Music Made Easy

For Americans who loved to listen to music at home, 1948 was an important year. Columbia Records released a new 12-inch vinyl record. These new records had smaller grooves and played at 33 1/3 revolutions per minute (rpm) instead of the previous 78 revolutions. They were called long-playing records, or LPs, because they offered twenty-five minutes of music per side instead of the three to five minutes of previous records. This meant they could contain several songs instead of just one or two. LPs boasted improved sound quality, so music lovers could feel almost as if they had a live band playing in their own home. LPs dominated music for more than thirty years until the arrival of compact discs.

Vinyl records changed the way the world heard music.

Jukebox Junkies

Teenagers in the forties had money to spend. So advertisers and manufacturers began to focus on this important market. Many teens held jobs to support the war effort, and on Saturday nights they liked to spend their money in dance halls. This provided a boost to the music industry. By 1946, record companies were selling ten times more songs than they had sold ten years earlier. The major studios, such as RCA and Decca, sold 100 million records each year. With the new long-playing 45-rpm and 33-rpm records, jukeboxes became a major industry. They brought in about 5 billion nickels each year. Teens could listen to jukebox music at their favorite soda shop before heading to the dance hall, where they practiced their lindy and jitterbug dance moves.

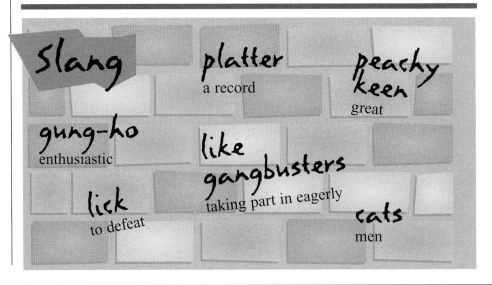

Slang

platter
a record

peachy keen
great

gung-ho
enthusiastic

like gangbusters
taking part in eagerly

lick
to defeat

cats
men

Dancing The Night Away

Despite the worry and fear brought by the war, Americans could lift their spirits at the dance halls. The jitterbug helped chase away the fears of American boys overseas, even if only for an evening. This swing dance had been popular in the 1930s but became a worldwide sensation in the forties. American servicemen spread the dance to the countries where they were stationed. It was a hit at home, too. Partners often held both hands and did different dance steps and acrobatic swings. They usually made up their own steps. This high-energy dance was best performed to the music of swing bands or their records. Even the musicians who played in dance halls every week could not say exactly which moves made up the jitterbug. Americans did not mind—they just wanted to spend their weekends spinning, flipping, and tapping their toes to hot forties swing music.

■ Many Saturday nights were spent dancing the jitterbug.

Risky Business

In 1946, many women looked to Louis Réard's invention to shake up their summer. Réard had created the two-piece bathing suit. Many people thought these bathing suits immodest because they did not cover nearly as much of women's bodies as previous suits. Others found the new suits liberating, not to mention attention-getting! Mediterranean beaches were the first to be invaded by two-piece suits, and the trend soon hit American shores. The suits were called bikinis. Their name came from the Bikini Atoll, which is an island in the South Pacific. Bikini is where Americans tested nuclear weapons. People said bikini suits caused as much commotion as the explosions.

SLUMBER PARTIES

■ In the 1940s, Friday nights were meant for friends. Nothing brought a group of girls closer than weekly sleep-overs. The teens dressed in their fathers' oversized pajamas or nightshirts and spent the evening talking. They discussed what they had read in teen magazines and took turns reading from their favorite articles. The girls did not neglect their beauty treatments during these parties. They still applied nightly mud masks to clear their skin and did their hair up in curlers or pins. The teens burned extra energy by having pillow fights before trying to sleep. These slumber parties were held across the country.

D-Day Arrives

The Allies had been planning D-Day for months. On June 6, 1944, 300,000 U.S., British, and Canadian troops landed on the beaches of Normandy, France. They attacked German strongholds. By the end of the day, the Allies had re-entered continental Europe. The cost of the attack was high: thousands had been killed or wounded. Still, this was a big step toward ending the war. During the following months, the Allies advanced across Europe. By April 1945, Germany had been defeated. Its leader, Adolf Hitler shot himself as Russian troops closed in to capture him. In May, Germany surrendered, and millions of people celebrated around the world. The Allies still had to stop Japan, though.

By this time, the U.S. had won many battles against Japan in the Pacific. Then, in early 1945, U.S. forces attacked the islands of Iwo Jima and Okinawa. A photograph of Marines raising the U.S. flag at Iwo Jima became a well-known image of the war. The cost of these two missions was high, and three of the six Marines in that photograph died before the battle was over. Japan did not

■ Allied forces storm the beaches of Normandy with hopes of ending the war.

surrender Iwo Jima until it had lost 20,000 of the 21,000 soldiers stationed there. Heavy resistance continued in Okinawa for three months before the island fell in June. The end of the Pacific conflict was close at hand.

The Start of the War

When Germany invaded Poland in 1939, the stage was set for World War II. Despite British and French efforts, the Germans took Poland easily. Hitler then turned on Norway and Denmark. He knew that to conquer the West, he needed to be strong in the north. There was fierce resistance to the German invasion in some parts of these countries, but although Britain and France sent forces to help, they could not stop Hitler. Soon, France

was under attack and Allied troops had to pull out. By June, France had fallen to Germany. Hitler next intended to conquer Britain. To weaken the country before invading it, German planes bombed Britain month after month. The Battle of Britain lasted from the summer of 1940 to May 1941. Britain's radar helped detect German planes, and many were shot down. Eventually, Hitler called off the invasion.

Hitler had formed alliances in Italy, the Soviet Union, and Japan. While Japanese troops spread across Asia, the other

Axis powers took over much of Eastern Europe. Meanwhile, Italian troops invaded Greece and fought the British in northern Africa.

Hitler had never intended to remain an ally of the Soviet Union. On June 22, 1941, Germany betrayed its pact with the Soviets and launched a surprise attack on the USSR. The Soviet Union soon joined the Allies and fought against Hitler for the rest of the war. The conflict involved countries around the world, earning the title of World War II.

THE HOLOCAUST

■ Adolf Hitler wanted to create a "master race" of superior people. He ordered all people he thought inferior to be captured and killed. Among other groups, Jewish people were targeted by Hitler and his Nazi followers. In 1942, Nazi officials met to decide how to deal with the "Jewish question." At the Wannsee Conference, they decided that all Jews in Europe would be taken to camps. Those in good health would be put to work as slaves. Those who could not work would be "appropriately dealt with"—they would be killed. Millions of Jews, Gypsies, and other "undesirables" were taken from their homes and forced into concentration camps, where many were gassed to death. Most of the victims were from Poland and the USSR. The horror of what was happening was discovered too late. Only after the war did the world learn the truth about the Jewish Holocaust.

"We have spent $2 billion on the greatest scientific gamble in history—and won."
President Harry Truman, after dropping the atomic bomb

■ The power of the atomic bomb was enough to destroy entire cities.

The Final Days of the War

The atomic bomb, which the U.S. had worked to create, was put to the test on August 6, 1945. A B-29 bomber dropped the bomb on Hiroshima, creating a blast that was two thousand times more powerful than any bomb known before. Within one second of the explosion, 80,000 Japanese people died. The temperature at the bomb's center reached 5,432° Fahrenheit. Many other people later died from exposure to **radiation**. President Truman demanded that Japan surrender or risk a "rain of ruin" from the sky. Japan ignored the warning. Three days later, another bomb fell, this time on Nagasaki. The blast killed 60,000 and secured Japan's surrender. World War II officially ended. The Allies were the victors, but nobody really won. More than 35 million people died in World War II.

Independent Israel

For years, David Ben-Gurion had pushed for a Jewish state ruled by Jewish, not British, people. In 1947, the United Nations (UN) voted to give Palestine independence from Britain. The area was split into a Jewish state and an Arab state. Arab countries immediately prepared to invade the new Jewish country called Israel.

May 14, 1948, marked the first day of Israel's independence. The following day, five Arab nations attacked it. The Israeli troops managed to defend their new country against these attackers, even though they were not as well armed. By the end of 1948, Israel had defeated Arab forces and taken about half of the land the UN had given to the Arabs. Arab countries refused to recognize Israel as a state or negotiate with its government. They vowed to destroy Israel and reclaim their land.

■ The Nuremberg trials held German Nazis accountable for war crimes.

War Criminals on Trial

Between November 1945 and October 1946, Nuremberg, Germany, was buzzing with the most important trials of the century. Twenty-four Nazi leaders were being held accountable for their actions during the war. They were charged with ordering and overseeing the murder of millions of people. The **tribunals** were led by the U.S., Britain, France, and the USSR. Many of the men on trial sat emotionless during the hearings. They felt they had done nothing wrong— they were just following orders. At times during the trials, some of the accused did not even bother to wear the earphones that translated the testimony into German.

By the end of the ordeal, one defendant had committed suicide, and another was declared unfit to stand trial. Three were found not guilty and released, and twelve were sentenced to death for their crimes. Three other accused were given life sentences, and the remaining four were given prison terms of between ten and twenty years. For many victims of the Holocaust, the punishment was not enough.

DEAD SEA SCROLLS

■ A man looking for his goat along the Dead Sea in Jordan found something amazing in 1947. He noticed a narrow opening in the limestone cliffs and decided to look inside. He found several **earthenware** jars. One jar held three leather scrolls wrapped in linen. These scrolls contained writing that gave the world a look into life 2,000 years before. For the next twenty years, people searched for more scrolls. Four nearby sites brought the scroll total to eight, plus tens of thousands of fragments dated between the third century BCE and CE 135. The finds included **biblical** texts that were 1,000 years older than any previously known texts.

Crying for Argentina

After a posting in Italy during the war, Colonel Juan Perón came home to Argentina with new ideas influenced by the Italian fascists. By 1945, this popular man was named vice president and war secretary. Some Argentineans did not agree with some of his ideas and methods. Perón was imprisoned by his opponents in 1945 but was freed after workers rallied in protest. The day he was freed, he announced that he would run for president. In the election, he won 52 percent of the vote and became president in 1946.

Perón passed laws that gave him absolute power. He raised wages, built hospitals, gave women the right to vote, and gave free medical care to citizens. People cheered Perón as a hero. His wife Eva (also called Evita) was even more popular—she was almost

Perón's goal was to make Argentina the most powerful country in Latin America.

worshiped. She helped charities and declared her love for Argentina. At the same time, her husband censored newspapers, destroyed opponents, and drove out professors and judges. His government was very corrupt.

In 1955, the military ousted him from power, and Perón was exiled to Spain. He returned in 1973 and was, once again, elected president. He held the post until his death in 1974.

Peaceful Resolutions

While the world was at war, Mohandas Gandhi was fighting against violence. He achieved his aims by inspiring people to take part in nonviolent protests. All of his victories were achieved without bloodshed. For twenty years, Gandhi had worked for the rights of Indians in South Africa. He returned home to India during World War I to press for independence from Britain. He became a symbol of an independent India and was called the Mahatma, meaning "great soul." After years of battling for his people and being jailed for his efforts, Gandhi saw India become independent in 1947. The country was split into India, which was mainly Hindu, and Pakistan, which was Muslim. Immediately, there was fighting between the two sides. Gandhi

begged people to live together peacefully. He tried to stop the violence by **fasting** until he was nearly dead. This act finally calmed the riots.

On January 30, 1948, Gandhi was walking to join about 500 people in evening prayer when

Gandhi offered peaceful solutions to violent problems.

an Indian citizen rushed forward and fired three shots at him. The man who had pushed for peace died by violence. He was 79 years old.

■ Protesters gather in Washington, DC, to lobby for civil rights.

Step Closer to Equal Rights

African Americans were fighting overseas to free people from oppression in 1941, but at home, they did not have the very rights they were fighting for on behalf of others. Civil rights activist and labor leader A. Phillip Randolph masterminded a march on Washington. He threatened to bring 50,000 protesters if job **discrimination** was not stopped.

President Roosevelt's wife, Eleanor, was an activist as well. She encouraged her husband to stop discrimination in war-industry jobs. He listened. He ordered defense plants to hire both African-American and white employees. On June 25, he created the Fair Employment Practices Committee to make sure these industries did not discriminate according to skin color.

F.D.R. A FIRST

■ In 1940, the country wondered what President Roosevelt would do. In 144 years, no president had run for a third term in office. For much of the year, the president remained tight-lipped about his plans. Then he said he would run against Republican Wendell Willkie. Willkie came across as a country bumpkin, in wrinkled suits, the same tie every day, and no watch. His boyish charm hid a brilliant mind. He was the toughest opponent Roosevelt had faced. The men agreed on many of the issues—they both supported aid to Britain against the Nazis, and both favored social reforms. The Republicans tried to make an issue out of the president seeking a third term, but with the war in Europe and the national income $40 billion above where it had been during the last Republican administration, the issue did not seem important. The November election lured a record 50 million Americans to the polls. Willkie won more than 22 million votes. This was more than any other Republican had received. Roosevelt, however, won 27 million votes and another term as president.

Lend-Lease Bill

In 1941, President Roosevelt introduced the Lend-Lease bill, which allowed aid to be given to any country that the president felt was important to the defense of the United States. The aid would not be cash. It would be goods or services. The president could choose any defense item and offer it to any country. This shocked Roosevelt's opponents. Roosevelt had more power than any other president before. After much debate, the U.S. public supported the measure. The bill passed on March 11, and $7 billion was put into the program. Britain was overjoyed. It received 951 military tanks from the U.S. By Christmas, food as well as trucks, guns, planes, and ammunition had been shipped to Britain. Not all Europeans appreciated the bill. The Italian government criticized it and said it would bring unpleasant surprises to Britain and the U.S. This proved correct. The U.S. built up its military stocks as it supplied Britain. The Axis powers viewed this as a threat. On December 7, 1941, Japan responded to the threat by bombing Pearl Harbor. This drew the U.S. into active battle in World War II.

America Inches Toward War

President Roosevelt tried to find a way to help defeat the Axis powers without going back on promises to not enter the war. Opinion polls showed that more Americans wanted to help Hitler's victims, even if it meant actively fighting. Roosevelt used this as a basis for lending Britain fifty old battleships in exchange for the right to build U.S. military bases on British territory. Then he signed the Selective Training and Services Act. This brought the first peacetime **conscription** to the country, promising that it would be used only to defend the U.S. The final nudge to join the war came on December 7, 1941, when Japanese airplanes attacked Pearl Harbor. The raid sank or damaged eight battleships and thirteen other naval vessels. The event brought Americans together, making them determined to fight to the finish. The day after the attack on Pearl Harbor, Congress voted 470 to 1 to join the war. Germany and Italy declared war on the U.S. on December 11.

■ The Japanese attack on Pearl Harbor thrust the U.S. into World War II.

WORLD FOCUS

NEW LEADERS FOR THE ALLIES

As the war **escalated**, some Allied countries began questioning their leaders. French President Edouard Daladier and British Prime Minister Neville Chamberlain had tried to keep Hitler happy to avoid a war. Their methods had not worked. Citizens looked for new people to pull them out of the conflict. In March 1940, the French asked finance minister Paul Reynaud to form the new government. He had more aggressive ideas about how to fight the Germans, but when Hitler invaded, France had outdated defenses and a government that was divided about whether they should keep fighting. The French were defeated, and Reynaud and many government officials were captured and put in Nazi concentration camps.

Britain, on the other hand, found success with its new leader. Winston Churchill became prime minister in May 1940. He became a symbol of British strength and determination. He inspired Britons to support the war wholeheartedly. He held his fingers in a "V" for "Victory" and believed it would happen. His people did not disappoint him.

Wartime President

On April 12, 1945, Harry Truman was sworn in as president after Franklin Roosevelt's death. The country was saddened by the passing of their longest-serving president, and Americans looked to Truman to carry on his efforts. Truman did just that. He continued to support the war and then helped negotiate peace. After the war, he worked on shifting the country's industrial focus from military to peacetime production. Early in his presidency, Truman made some unpopular decisions. He brought the armed forces together under a civilian secretary of defense. Next, he ordered that the military mix African-American and white soldiers in the units. By election time, Truman had offended many members of his own party. His efforts to give more rights to African Americans angered his southern supporters. There was discontent throughout the party, and many people thought his opponent, Thomas Dewey, would win. Truman campaigned hard, making as many as sixteen speeches in a day. When the votes were counted, Truman had beat out Dewey by more than 2 million votes.

President Franklin Roosevelt fought for social reforms.

Before the U.S. even entered the war, President Roosevelt had met with Prime Minister Churchill on a warship off the coast of Newfoundland, Canada. The two issued the Atlantic Charter on August 14, 1941. This charter stated that people had the right to choose their own form of government. It said that every nation, regardless of its role in the war, had the right to the natural resources it needed. The charter also called for better economic conditions, with fair treatment of workers, freedom to sail the seas, and "freedom from fear."

At a conference on January 1, 1942, the countries at war with the Axis powers agreed to the principles in the Atlantic Charter. The United Nations Declaration would become the basis of the UN.

> "The remedy lies in breaking the vicious circle and restoring the confidence of the European people in the economic future of...Europe as a whole."
>
> George Marshall

Marshall Plan in Effect

Europe was in a desperate state after being ravaged by war for six years. President Truman decided to help rebuild Europe and protect it from the USSR. He and Secretary of State George C. Marshall created the European Recovery Plan, also known as the Marshall Plan. A strong European market would benefit U.S. trade as well as strengthen democracy in Western Europe. The U.S. government also wanted to make West Germany (which was occupied by U.S., British, and French troops) a part of democratic Europe. In June 1947, Marshall announced that the U.S. would help pay for a long-term rebuilding effort in Europe. The U.S. spent more than $12.5 billion over four years to rebuild Europe. This prompted the Soviet government to bring together the communist states of Eastern Europe.

Post War

In September 1945, President Truman started changing the U.S. economy from one of war to one of peace. He asked Congress for a liberal economic recovery program. This twenty-one point program called for a job for every American, unemployment benefits, cooperation between workers and management, and housing subsidies. He said that everyone in the country deserved and should expect a "Fair Deal." For most, this meant jobs for the servicemen. To many women, it meant the loss of their jobs to the men returning from war. Truman was accused

Although many of his ideas were met with resistance, Truman continued to press for civil rights.

of ignoring women in his Fair Deal program. Truman replaced the War Labor Board with the Wage Stabilization Board in December 1945. Food, shoe, and tire rationing was finally over. There was a huge demand for

housing and for more jobs now that "our boys" were back from overseas. In 1946, Truman was concerned about a possible recession after the war boom. Congress passed the Employment Act to prevent a recession from developing into a depression. The Act created a Council of Economic Advisors who studied the economy, pinpointed weaknesses, and offered suggestions on how to keep the economy stable. The economy was picking up and life was, at last, getting back to normal.

Each of the "Hollywood Ten" served time in prison.

Hollywood Under Fire

The Cold War that was brewing between the USSR and the U.S. seeped into society. In 1947, the House Committee on Un-American Activities (HUAC) heard from celebrities who said the movie industry was full of communists. The committee then called dozens of actors and directors to appear before it to defend themselves.

The hearings began in October. Eleven writers, producers, and directors refused to answer questions about whether they were or had ever been communists. The First Amendment gave them the right of political freedom. Playwright Bertolt Brecht left the U.S. for Switzerland the day after he testified. The remaining rebels became known as the "Hollywood Ten." All ten men were charged with contempt for not cooperating and were sentenced to between four and ten months in prison. Only one of the ten went back on his refusal to answer. He was allowed to continue working. Others lost their careers or worked under false names.

SALESMAN TRAGEDY

■ Playwright Arthur Miller wanted to write a classic tragedy in a modern-day context. The result was *Death of a Salesman* in 1949. Miller tells the story of Willy Loman, an aging traveling salesman who loses his job. All his life, Loman waited for things to get better, but they never did. Throughout the play, Willy has to accept his own failures in life along with the failures of his two sons. Like many other tragic heroes, he commits suicide. The play won Miller the Pulitzer Prize for Drama and the New York Drama Critics' Circle Award for best play of the year.

■ Richard Wright's *Native Son* is a literary masterpiece.

Bestseller

African American Richard Wright was a best-selling author and a communist. His novel *Native Son* (1940) was an instant hit. The story follows Bigger Thomas, an African American who accidentally suffocates his white employer's daughter. He then kills his own girlfriend when police close in on him, and he ends up on death row. The novel struck a chord with Americans and influenced many young writers. Wright was the first African American to write a bestseller, and he was one of the most effective spokespeople for racial equality in his generation. He wanted America to know how angry African Americans were about the way they were treated. After writing a best-selling autobiography, *Black Boy* (1945), Wright moved to Paris. He claimed that there was more freedom in a city block in Paris than there was in the entire U.S.

McCullers Hunts Down Acclaim

Many people think that Carson McCullers's first novel was her best. She wrote *The Heart Is a Lonely Hunter* (1940) when she was only 23 years old. The novel follows life in a small, southern town through the eyes of a young girl who can neither speak nor hear. She finds a friend in another young girl. The novel explores themes of loneliness and the need for human love and contact. McCullers relied on memories of her own childhood for much of her writing. Her compassion and sensitivity toward the lonely and outcast shines through in her novels and stories. Her later novels, *Reflections in a Golden Eye* (1941) and *The Member of the Wedding* (1946), were also popular. Each of these three novels was made into a movie. McCullers also wrote short stories and plays that brought her praise in the U.S. and around the world.

W🜨RLD FOCUS

BIG BROTHER

In 1949, Eric Blair's impression of the future hit American streets. The novelist, who wrote under the name George Orwell, told of a future 1984, in which freedom, beauty, privacy, and independent thought are not allowed. In the novel, citizens live under the watchful eye of Big Brother. Any mistake or attempt to be an individual can be reported to the thought police. The hero of the book creates propaganda for the Ministry of Truth. He rebels against the system and falls in love with a co-worker who shares his ideas. Big Brother does not allow such disrespect, and the hero is captured, tortured, and "re-educated."

Blair's experiences fighting in the Spanish Civil War influenced his writing and caused him to criticize the communist system. This criticism can be seen in 1984 as well as in Animal Farm *(1945).* Animal Farm *is a political story about barnyard animals who defeat their human oppressors only to be oppressed by the pigs among them. This novel contributed to Blair's success, but* 1984 *made him famous. He did not live long enough to see how far-reaching his novel became. He died of* **tuberculosis** *at the age of forty-six—six months after the book was published.*

WILL ECSTASY BE A CRIME ...IN THE TERRIFYING WORLD OF THE FUTURE?

Amazing wonders of tomorrow! Nothing like it ever filmed! FROM THE STARTLING GEORGE ORWELL NOVEL

ANTI-SEX LEAGUE

"1984"

EDMOND O'BRIEN · MICHAEL REDGRAVE · JAN STERLING

Screenplay by WILLIAM P. TEMPLETON and RALPH BETTINSON · From the Book by GEORGE ORWELL

■ After its success as a novel, *1984* was made into a movie.

War Novel a Hit

Norman Mailer's first novel made him an instant success. The 25-year-old's war novel, *The Naked and the Dead*, was published in 1948. The book is based on Mailer's experiences in World War II and is about an army platoon's invasion of Japan. The novel is cynical but honest. Many Americans who were feeling angry about the war related to Mailer's writing. *The Naked and the Dead* was immediately dubbed "the greatest U.S. book to come out of the war." Mailer was a celebrity. His later books, however, were always compared to his first great achievement. Critics were often disappointed. Mailer wrote several novels, including *Barbary Shore* (1951), *The Deer Park* (1955), *The American Dream* (1965) and *Why Are We in Vietnam?* (1967). Many of his novels and essays explored violence in American society.

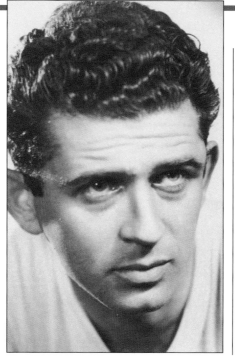

■ Norman Mailer's writings are a plea for peace.

MONTICELLO PUBLIC LIBRARY
512 E. LAKE AVE.
MONTICELLO, WI 53570

Manhattan Project

In 1942, the U.S. government decided that people doing research on nuclear weapons should combine their efforts. Physicist J. Robert Oppenheimer and Brigadier General Leslie R. Groves worked together to lead the Manhattan Project, named for the location of its headquarters. About 100,000 people and a dozen university laboratories contributed to the research. Top scientists were then invited to a secret New Mexico compound to help develop nuclear weapons. Oppenheimer handled the scientific side of the project, and Groves was in charge of the staff and defense of the site. Less than three years later, the efforts paid off. A test explosion flashed brilliant light across the desert. Oppenheimer was concerned about the effects of this weapon, seeing it as the "shatterer of worlds." Groves was excited. The project could end the war. Their research would be applied to create the most devastating weapon in history—the atomic bomb.

Yeager Breaks Barrier

Before 1947, the speed of sound seemed too fast to imagine. When a plane flies slower than the speed of sound, it sends sound waves ahead of it. As the plane nears the speed of sound, these waves can cause pressure and spin the plane out of control. In October, Charles Yeager, one of the country's best fighter pilots, boarded the Bell X-1 plane to attempt to break the sound barrier. This research plane was designed to reduce the amount of pressure on it. The bullet-shaped design was a success. The 24-year-old pilot reached speeds of 700 miles an hour—or Mach 1.06—at 43,000 feet in the air. Despite two broken ribs from an accident the night before, Yeager became the first person to fly faster than the speed of sound.

Breaking the sound barrier made Chuck Yeager a part of aviation history.

DANGEROUS ELEMENTS

In 1940, U.S. scientists discovered plutonium. This element would later be used in the first nuclear weapon. The weapon that would bring down the Axis powers was made possible, ironically, by the work of Germans. Two German scientists had bombarded uranium with neutrons. They later discovered how to split the uranium atom in two. American scientists took the experiment further and found how to produce plutonium. This new element could be split easier and faster than uranium. This meant that when used in weapons, it was very powerful. Just 300 grams of plutonium could create an explosion equal to 20,000 tons of dynamite.

Transistors Revolutionize Electronics

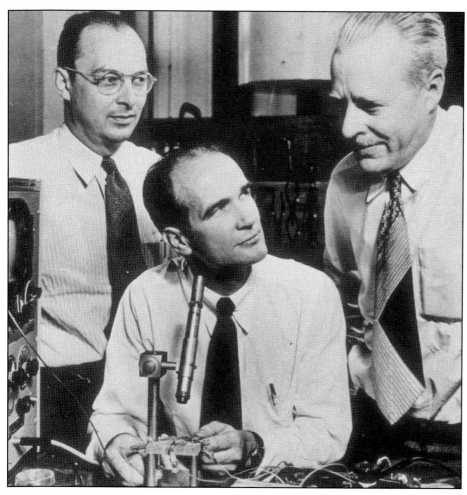
■ The invention of the transistor changed the way radios are made.

In 1947, William Shockley invited some colleagues at Bell Telephone Laboratories to look at the result of his experiments. Shockley and co-researchers John Bardeen and Walter Brattain showed how an electric current could pass through a tiny device called a transistor. Their discovery put an end to Bell's glass-enclosed vacuum tubes, which had been used until that time. Transistors were inexpensive to produce, long-lasting, did not require much power, and did not create as much heat as vacuum tubes did.

When the discovery was made public, electronics experts were excited by the possibilities. Within a decade, transistor radios that could fit in a pocket demonstrated how far the invention had come. Brattain, Shockley, and Bardeen were awarded the Nobel Prize for Physics in 1956.

Tuberculosis Controlled

By 1944, penicillin was helping people fight infections. It was not, however, effective against the disease tuberculosis (TB). In January 1944, microbiologist Selman Waksman announced his discovery of a new antibiotic called streptomycin. Testing confirmed that it worked well against tuberculosis. This discovery changed the treatment of TB forever—doctors could attack the disease rather than the symptoms. Scientists soon discovered that streptomycin was not enough to fight TB on its own. Still, it worked well when combined with other antibiotics. The resulting drug was so effective that within five years of introducing it, TB rates dropped dramatically in many parts of the world.

ENIAC Built

In 1946, scientists at the University of Pennsylvania created the world's first all-purpose electronic digital computer. The machine, called the Electronic Numerical Integrator and Computer, or ENIAC, weighed 30 tons and contained 18,000 vacuum tubes. It was built to perform **ballistic** equations for the U.S. Army. ENIAC was installed at Aberdeen, Maryland. Despite its enormous size, ENIAC was an improvement over previous computers. The machine could solve 5,000 mathematical operations per second. People in the science community were excited by what ENIAC could mean for the future. A magazine predicted that computers in years to come might have only 1,000 tubes and might weigh no more than 1.5 tons.

Girls of Summer

Hundreds of Major League players joined the military during the 1940s. In 1943, Chicago Cubs owner Phillip Wrigley founded the All American Girls' Professional Baseball League (AAGPBL). Teams from across the Midwest competed in major-league parks, and their popularity soared. Fans soon realized that the girls could really play, and thousands paid to watch their favorite teams. The players had special rules. Each player attended charm school, where she learned beauty tips and **etiquette**. The rules stated that she always had to be dressed in feminine clothes off the diamond—no pants or shorts. Long hair was preferred, and lipstick was a must. On the field, players had to wear baseball skirts rather than pants, a style that offered no protection for women's legs when they slid into a base or dove after a ball. Other than these rules, the women's

The women of the AAGPBL took the baseball world by storm.

game was very similar to the men's. Women used a smaller ball and a shortened field. They started out pitching underhand, but by 1948, pitchers were throwing overhand. The game was exciting and outlasted the return of U.S. soldiers and baseball players. This did not last for long, though. Televised baseball games and financial problems led to the AAGPBL's end. The league was dissolved in 1954, but it remains a unique part of baseball history.

Bears Dominate

The Chicago Bears began the decade with a championship win over the Washington Redskins. The "T" formation created by the coaches offered the quarterback protection and allowed for an easy hand-off. This prevented the Redskins from scoring.

The Bears, including Sid Luckman and Harry Clark, defended their title in 1941 against the New York Giants. The following year, they finished the regular season without a loss but lost the play-off championship to the Redskins, 14 to 6. In 1943, the team fought back to the top. With

George Blanda's kicking ability helped propel the Chicago Bears to victory.

Sid Luckman's leadership, the team reclaimed the championship in a victory over Washington. Washington's Sammy Baugh gave the game his all—in 1943, he became the first player to intercept four passes in a game. Still, he could not compete with Luckman's arm. Luckman was the first professional player to pass for more than 400 yards in a single game. After two years of not making the finals, the Bears returned to take back the championship. In 1946, Sid Luckman and Ken Kavanaugh led the team to victory over the Giants. The Bears would have to wait until 1963 before they would win another championship.

Olympic Heroes

The Olympic Games scheduled for 1940 and 1944 were cancelled because of the war. Many members of the International Olympic Committee felt that the 1948 Games should be cancelled as well. The things that had happened during the war went against the Olympic ideal of universal peace. Despite these concerns, London, England, still recovering from the war, hosted the Summer Games in August. The Olympics were a huge success, especially for U.S. athletes. They chalked up 662 points and 38 gold medals. Second-place Sweden trailed with only 353 points. Bob Mathias proved to be one of the biggest stars of the Games. The 17-year-old decathlete endured a **grueling** contest to take home the gold.

The 1948 Winter Olympic Games in Saint Moritz, Switzerland, also brought medals home to the U.S. At the Games, Dick Button became the first American to win an Olympic gold medal in figure skating, and Gretchen Fraser became the first American to take home Olympic medals in alpine skiing. She won a gold medal in slalom and a silver in the alpine combined competition.

■ Gretchen Fraser led the Olympic skiing charge.

New Basketball League

In 1946, a group of New York executives created a new professional basketball league called the Basketball Association of America (BAA). This new league had teams in New York City, Boston, Philadelphia, Chicago, and Detroit. It competed with the National Basketball League (NBL), which had been established in the mid-thirties. Just as the 1948 season was about to begin, the four best teams in the NBL—Minneapolis, Rochester, Fort Wayne, and Indianapolis—joined the BAA. The following year, the six remaining teams switched to the BAA. A three-division league called the National Basketball Association (NBA) was created. In 1949, the Minneapolis Lakers was the first team to win the new NBA championship title. In 1950, the NBA cut its size so that the teams would fit into two divisions. These later became the Eastern and Western conferences that were established in 1970. The NBA remained strong throughout the rest of the century.

King of Diamonds

Joltin' Joe DiMaggio was tearing up the base paths in 1941. The New York Yankee outfielder hit safely in fifty-six straight games. His streak ended with a double play in the eighth inning on July 17. DiMaggio finished that season with thirty home runs and 125 runs batted in. He was a leader, often being at the top of the league in batting, home runs, and runs batted in. DiMaggio was more than a great hitter—he was also one of the best outfielders ever to play the game. His strong skills led the Yankees to nine World Series titles, including the championship in 1941, 1947, and 1949. He was named Most Valuable Player of the American League in 1939, 1941, and 1947. Joltin' Joe played for the Yankees from his rookie year in 1936 until his retirement in 1952, except for the three years he spent serving in the Army.

America's fascination with this quiet hero did not end with his retirement from baseball. He captured the country's imagination when he married screen goddess Marilyn Monroe in 1954. They divorced later that year. DiMaggio had a big impact on U.S. society and culture. Even after his death in 1999, he remains a baseball legend and a hero to many.

■ Joltin' Joe DiMaggio ruled the diamond for more than two-and-a-half decades.

Joe Louis Heavyweight Champion

Joe Louis, nicknamed "The Brown Bomber," won his first professional boxing match with a knockout in 1934. Three years later, he fought his way to the top as the heavyweight champion. During his career, Louis won sixty-eight fights and only lost three. Fifty-four of these victories were by knockout. One especially tough loss was to German boxer Max Schmeling in 1936. The Nazis used the win to argue Nazi superiority. In a rematch two years later, Louis made his country proud by winning the bout in one round. The country celebrated, and Louis was a hero. He became a champion of the war, giving inspiring speeches and helping the government recruit people for service. The competition for the championship title was suspended in 1942—Louis had volunteered for service. "The Brown Bomber" hung up his gloves in 1949 after eleven years as boxing's heavyweight champion. He had defended his title twenty-five times. At 35 years old, Louis did not have the powerful jab and hook that once struck fear into his opponents. After losing to Rocky Marciano in a 1951 comeback, Lewis retired from boxing for good.

■ A young Joe Louis stands his ground.

Fantastic Footballer

Many people say that Don Hutson was the first true wide receiver in National Football League history. He signed with the Green Bay Packers in 1935 and enjoyed playing for one of the few teams that focused on passing the ball rather than running it down the field. His first professional play had him catching an 83-yard touchdown pass. Opposing players soon came to fear Hutson. He became the first player to be covered by several defenders at the same time. With Hutson at the helm, the Packers battled to four division titles, including one in 1944, and two NFL championships. In 1942, Hutson set the league season scoring record with 138 points. In the Green Bay Packers star's eleven-year career, he was the league's top scorer five times and its best receiver eight times. He netted top honors as the Most Valuable Player in 1941 and 1942. When he retired in 1945, he had 488 career catches, 7,991 yards, and 99 touchdowns to his name. Hutson was made a member of the Football Hall of Fame when it was established in 1963.

■ Jackie Robinson rallied against the obstacles of racism.

Breaking the Color Barrier

On April 15, 1947, in front of 26,500 fans, Jackie Robinson became the first African American to play in the major leagues. The road was not easy. Many of his teammates petitioned to have him removed from the field. There was talk that some teams would refuse to play the Dodgers if Robinson was in the game. As Robinson blazed around the bases, his opponents tried to **spike** him. He received death threats, and people often yelled at him. Despite these distractions, Robinson was named National League Rookie of the Year and led his team to the World Series.

It did not take long for Robinson to prove himself a star. His batting was consistently great, he played many positions well, and he was one of the most talented base runners in the game. In 1949, he was named the Most Valuable Player, and other African Americans began joining major league teams. In 1962, Robinson became the first African American inducted into the Baseball Hall of Fame.

WOMEN'S CLUBS

■ In the 1940s, millions of women across the country belonged to clubs. They met every week to discuss politics, the government, how to preserve historic monuments, and many other things. They banded together to try to have an impact on worthwhile issues. Some clubs enrolled women in "enriching study courses," such as Spanish lessons, singing, creative art, and handicrafts. Throughout the decade, these women met and served on committees that they hoped would make life in the U.S. better. Groups such as the National Association of Colored Women's Clubs (NACWC) were key players in the war effort and the civil rights movement.

Woman Power

The war overseas was fought mostly by men. At home, the war was fought mostly by women. As men left to fight, women took over their jobs in factories and businesses. At first, single women were hired. As more U.S. men left for active duty, married women were added to the workforce. By 1944, about 3.5 million women stood alongside 6 million men on factory assembly lines. War goods, including planes, ships, and ammunition, were produced in great numbers by women. After the war, when the men returned to the U.S., the

■ U.S. women assemble guns for the Allied war effort.

women were expected to step aside. Many women did not want to stop working and fought to keep their jobs.

During the war, some women joined the Women's Auxilliary Army Corps to help the war effort more directly. This branch of the military was established in May 1942. Congress also set up women's corps in the navy and other branches of the forces. About 350,000 women served in all military areas except combat.

Restrictions and Rations

The entire country was expected to do its part to help troops overseas. Americans turned in scrap metal to be made into weapons, and they saved bacon grease for use when making ammunition. They saved cans and newspapers, too. Doing their part also meant obeying the rules about rationed goods. In January 1942, Americans were given books and stamps that showed what food they could buy and how much. The books were confusing, and many Americans could not make sense of what they were expected to do—different

colored tokens were worth a different number of points, and some could be used to make change, while others could not. People tried to follow the rules, although they accepted sugar, meat, and coffee rationing better than gasoline rationing. Many

people did not think that 3 gallons per week was enough. Some tried to manufacture fake cards for gas, but most stayed within the limits. Despite the restrictions, Americans were better fed in 1945 than ever before.

Wartime Shopping Guide	
Hamburger (1 pound)	7 points
Butter (1 pound)	16 points
Ham (1 pound)	7 points
Cheddar cheese (1 pound)	8 points
Pineapple juice (46 ounces)	22 points
Ketchup (14 ounces)	15 points
Carrots (16 ounces)	6 points

Japanese Americans Interned

After the attack on Pearl Harbor, many Americans did not trust citizens of Japanese origin. They feared that these people, especially those in coastal areas, would help the Japanese attackers. In 1942, the military forced all Japanese residents on the West Coast to move to detention centers inland. About 110,000 Japanese Americans were moved during the war, long after any threat from Japan was gone. Yet about 17,600 Japanese Americans joined the armed forces and fought hard for their country—the U.S.

■ Taken from their home, a family of Japanese Americans prepares for life in a detention camp.

A Hero's Welcome

During the war, Americans hailed some remarkable and brave soldiers as heroes. Some of these men were awarded the Congressional Medal of Honor, the highest honor for bravery. One hero, Lieutenant David Waybur, was badly injured. Even so, he destroyed an Italian tank and kept three others at bay long enough for help to arrive. Another was Commander Howard Gilmore, whose submarine was caught on the surface by a Japanese gunboat. Gilmore rammed and disabled the gunboat. His submarine was ready to dive and the Japanese fired their guns. Gilmore was hit.

His crew tried to help him, but Gilmore ordered the submarine to dive. He knew he would die,

"No soldier ever survives a war."

Audie Murphy, in *To Hell and Back*

■ Lieutenant Audie Murphy received many honors for his bravery and heroism.

but it was his duty to save his ship and its crew.

Another famous hero was Lieutenant Audie Murphy, who earned the Legion of Merit and the Congressional Medal of Honor. He went on to appear in Hollywood movies, including one based on his book *To Hell and Back*, which describes his wartime experiences.

Battling Inflation

America did not fall into a depression after the war as many predicted. This was partly due to the high demand for goods that people had gone without in the war years. The real threat was inflation. The nation was reeling under wage and price controls. Business managers beat the system on the black markets. Workers fought against controls by striking. President Truman tried to stabilize the economy. He asked for permission to draft strikers into the army. The Senate rejected this request. Congress then enlarged the Office of Price Administration, but its authority was so diluted that Truman **vetoed** the move. In July 1946, there were no price or wage controls in the country. Prices soared by more than 25 percent. Congress moved quickly to pass another bill restricting this freedom, but the damage to consumers' pocketbooks was done. Luckily, supply soon caught up with demand. The average inflation rate without controls settled at around 6 percent. President Truman continued his fight to rebuild the economy after being re-elected in 1948.

"We believe that our economic system should rest on a democratic foundation and that wealth should be created for the benefit of all."

President Truman's State of the Union message, introducing his Fair Deal

■ Consumers protest the high costs of inflation.

War Production

In 1941, only 15 percent of U.S. industry was producing military items. Military spending was about $2 billion per month. By the early to mid-1940s, much of the economy was focused on the war. Many companies stopped business as usual and began producing materials needed to fight the war in Europe. President Roosevelt set high quotas to be met for 1942. He wanted 60,000 planes, 45,000 tanks, and 20,000 anti-aircraft guns. In the first six months of 1942, the government spent more than $100 billion on war contracts. There were more goods on order than the economy had ever produced in one year. Now, about 33 percent of the economy was devoted to military production. The U.S. had a huge store of weapons and army vehicles. Toward the end of the war, defense plants were told to stop producing items such as anti-tank guns and trainer planes. Despite the large number of war products made in the U.S. during World War II, they accounted for only 40 percent of the gross national product.

WAR PRODUCTION FROM 1940 TO 1945	NUMBER
Small arms ammunition	41,585,000,000
Small arms	20,086,061
Aircraft bombs (tons)	5,822,000
Tanks and self-propelled guns	1,023,514
Artillery	372,431
Aircraft	296,429
Trucks	245,596
Naval ships	71,062
Cargo ships	5,425

Workers Strike

The war overseas was over, but there was a war at home to fight. Industries had made a great deal of money from the war. After the war, many workers were laid off. Because of this and other reasons, 4.5 million workers went on strike in 1946.

 Traffic came to a standstill as workers across the nation went on strike.

This brought the coal, steel, automobile, and electric industries to their knees. There were about 113 million worker-days lost due to the striking. Still, the strikers brought with them the new peace, and the strikes were nonviolent.

MONEY TROUBLES

During the war years, Roosevelt's government spent more than $320 billion. Taxation brought about $130 billion into the wartime economy. The rest of the money came from borrowing from other countries. In 1944 alone, the government created a debt of more than $50 billion—more than twice the country's total debt in 1941. By the end of the war, the debt had ballooned to about $280 billion. This was almost six times larger than when Pearl Harbor was attacked.

With the fighting over, the government had to find a way to reduce the debt, provide jobs, and rebuild after the massive spending of the previous years.

Truman's Fair Deal

President Truman had a Democratic Congress, but his Fair Deal program was met with resistance. Congress approved some of Truman's proposals but rejected others. The public housing bill, increased social security coverage, and higher minimum wage were approved by Congress. So were the Fair Deal's proposals for more subsidies for farmers, flood control, and **rural electrification**. Congress opposed Truman's proposals to construct the St. Lawrence Seaway and create several public hydroelectric companies.

Congress also rejected Truman's civil rights proposals, which included an anti-**lynching** law. Truman was disappointed by the rejection, but he was not discouraged.

He strengthened civil rights through his actions with the Justice Department, and he appointed African Americans to high offices.

Young Fashions

Young people borrowed some fashions from the military. Many young men would not leave the house without their army boots. Boys and girls chose blue jeans, a necessity for defense workers. They liked the jeans baggy, and many girls rolled the pant legs up to just below their knees. Some girls even painted pictures of hearts, flowers, and horses on their jeans. Boys who did not wear army boots often liked to show off their loafers with their jeans rolled up a few inches, too. Boys and girls wore their shirts baggy and rarely tucked in. Some boys wore their letterman jackets or cardigans to show their school and team pride. Another fashion craze was striped football socks. These thick, knee-high socks worn by football players were a must with a skirt and loafers. Other teenagers wore mismatched shoes and socks as a fashion statement. For going out on dates, girls dressed up. They wore Stadium Girl lipstick and make-up, and looked to the many teen magazines for advice.

Fashion Led By War

The war interfered with forties fashions. U.S. designers based many of their fashions on military uniforms. The "Eisenhower" jacket had shoulder pads and a drawstring waist. Berets and army hats were a hit with women. As the war dragged on, there was a shortage of material, so hemlines rose to save on fabric. Since metal used to make zippers was needed for the war, designers met the challenge with wraparound skirts.

Fashion kept up with women's lifestyles. Women across the country were working, so the dresses and formal suits in their wardrobes were no longer practical. Casual clothing became popular, and short hair was all the rage. Women kept their hair short because long hair got in the way when they were working in factories. Short hair was still feminine, because many women kept their curls and waves intact. Those who chose to keep their hair long often pulled it back with a scarf or piled it on top of their head. Once the war was finally over, many women were eager for feminine, shapely styles again.

■ Although boxy, demob suits could be found on men from coast to coast.

New Duds for Men

At the end of the war, men's styles changed dramatically. Many soldiers who had returned to the U.S. had changed a great deal, too. They had left home as boys, and they came home as men, with bodies that would not fit into their old clothes. As troops were **demobilized**, the government gave each soldier a civilian suit to wear. These were dubbed "demob suits." Each man also was given a tie, a shirt, shoes, and a raincoat in which to re-enter civilian life. Some did not like the suits. They criticized the quality and insisted they were too boxy to be fashionable. Despite this, many men continued to wear demob suits for many years after the war.

Pedal Pushers

In the forties, most young people wore pants because of their factory and war jobs. Fashion designers changed their styles to fit this trend and other new habits. Teenagers often got around town on bicycles. Flowing skirts were impractical and a nuisance while on a bike. The rise of this hobby changed how some teens dressed. Pants called "pedal pushers" became popular in the forties. Pedal pushers were mid-calf length—they were either cut that length or rolled up. They were often worn with ankle socks rolled down. Pedal pushers made bicycle riding easier because the pants did not get caught in the spokes. The style was light and fun, something Americans were looking for during the war years. While teens started this fad, adults followed their lead throughout the decade. Pedal pushers were worn well into the 1950s by adults as well as teens.

Fashionable Science

A breakthrough in science led to a fashion must in the 1940s. A synthesized material called nylon had been created in 1934. By 1939, nylon stockings were being produced. These nylons had a seam running down the back of the leg. In the first year, 64 million pairs of nylons were sold to U.S women. There were near-riots in stores as women scrambled to get a pair for themselves. The war made nylon a rare find. Many U.S. women adapted to the shortage and drew a seam down the back of their bare legs to give the illusion of nylons. Other advancements in fabric soon followed.

In 1941, scientists invented an amazing fiber called Terylene. When woven, knitted, or blended with wool or cotton, this fabric would not stretch, fade, wrinkle, or get eaten by insects. After the war, Du Pont brought the fabric to the U.S. as Dacron.

NEW LOOKS

After the war, many American women craved a fashion that would recognize their femininity. In 1947, designer Christian Dior shook off the remnants of years of war style with his "New Look." The hemlines that had been forced up because of rationing were let down again. The look was elegant—long flowing skirts, narrow-shouldered jackets, and tight waistlines. After years of wearing coveralls and men's styles, this softer look celebrated femininity. No woman's wardrobe was complete without at least one "New Look" outfit. Dior's design house continued to set fashion trends for more than fifty-five years.

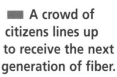 A crowd of citizens lines up to receive the next generation of fiber.

Braceros Introduced to American Agriculture

The Depression really was over. The "Depression Okies" who used to work on farms left those jobs for better-paying ones, usually in factories. So in 1942, fruit and crop growers asked the government for permission to import temporary workers from other countries. U.S. government officials met with Mexican authorities to discuss such an arrangement. Agricultural workers, referred to as braceros, who came to the U.S. to work would be given the same protection as any American worker, including wages. The labor unions fought against using temporary immigrants because they did not belong to a union. The unions accepted it as a wartime measure, but they were unhappy to see it carry on after the war. More than 200,000 temporary workers took agricultural jobs between 1942 and 1947.

■ Braceros wave from a train on their way to a U.S. farm.

Immigrants Flee Nazis

Many immigrants wanted to come to the U.S. in the forties. In December 1943, thousands of people trying to escape Hitler's Nazis arrived in the U.S. looking for new homes. These refugees claimed that they were being persecuted in Europe, and said they would die if they returned. The U.S. government believed them, and they were admitted to the U.S. At least 60,000 people had arrived in the country this way since 1933. Many of these refugees were Jewish people. They included scientist Albert Einstein, who arrived in 1933, and the composer Kurt Weill, who came in 1935. By 1950, about 200,000 displaced people had come to the U.S. for a fresh start after surviving the horrors of war.

New Policies

Immigration changed a great deal because of the war. After the conflict, Congress recognized two new immigration categories. In 1945, the War Brides Act allowed foreign-born wives, children, and fiancées of U.S. military stationed overseas to be admitted to the nation. Congress also made a special exception for refugees. These people were fleeing their homes for political reasons. They included people who had survived the Holocaust and the war, as well as those trying to flee the communism that was spreading across Eastern Europe after the war. Also included were Chinese refugees who were trying to escape the civil war raging in their country.

IMMIGRATION IN LARGE NUMBERS

Many people from all over the world applied for, and were granted, immigrant status in the U.S. during the 1940s. The list below shows where some of these people came from:

Germany	226,600
Canada	171,700
Great Britain	139,300
Mexico	60,600
Italy	57,700
Caribbean	49,700
Cuba	26,300
Austria	24,900
South America	21,800
Central America	21,700
Ireland	19,800
Oceania	14,600
Sweden	10,700
Norway	10,100
China	9,700
Africa	7,400

For immigrants, the Statue of Liberty symbolizes a new life in the U.S.

Asian Immigration

In 1943, the Magnuson Act was passed. Since 1882, no Chinese people had been allowed into the U.S. The Magnuson Act allowed 105 to come each year.

East Indians were also given immigration opportunities in the 1940s. At the start of the decade, there were only about 2,400 East Indians in the U.S. In 1946, Congress passed the Luce-Cellar Act. This removed the "barred zone" clause of the 1917 Act and allowed people from India to enter the U.S. and become citizens. Like the Magnuson Act, the Luce-Cellar Act allowed a small number of immigrants per year—only 105 East Indians were accepted. When India became independent, the quotas reflected this change, allowing for 105 immigrants for each of India, Pakistan, Sri Lanka, and Burma.

War Tunes

In 1942, composer Frank Loesser heard about a chaplain stationed at Pearl Harbor. He had told his congregation to "praise the Lord and pass the ammunition." These words gave Loesser the idea for his hit song of the same name. He later won an Academy Award for "Baby, It's Cold Outside." After serving in the war himself, Loesser found fame with his popular stage musicals, including *Guys and Dolls*.

The Andrews Sisters also did their part to help keep up morale in the forties. Allied troops and Americans loved this trio. The singers constantly entertained soldiers during the war. With hits such as "Don't Sit Under the Apple Tree (With Anyone Else But Me)" and "Boogie Woogie Bugle Boy," the sisters helped keep people cheerful during the hardships of war. The Andrews Sisters' devotion to raising morale earned them the nickname "America's Wartime Sweethearts." Throughout their careers, the Andrews Sisters sold more than 90 million records and recorded more than 1,800 songs.

The Andrews Sisters sing "You're a Lucky Fellow, Mr. Smith" in *Buck Privates* (1941).

Million-Selling Miller

In 1941, Americans were moved by swing music. Big-band leaders, including Duke Ellington, Artie Shaw, the Dorsey brothers, Benny Goodman, and Count Basie, traveled the country's dance halls with their swing bands. In the forties, Glenn Miller proved that he and his orchestra were the tops. They were favorites for their pop songs and dance numbers. In 1941, they released *Sun Valley Serenade*, a movie about the band featuring their new song "Chattanooga Choo-Choo." The song rocketed to the top of the charts, selling a million copies. The record label, RCA, presented the band with a gold-plated copy of the record to show the company's appreciation. Miller's jazzy, danceable songs caught on like wildfire. "Pennsylvania 6-5000" and "In the Mood" put them on top. In 1942, Miller volunteered to lead the U.S. Army Air Force Band in Europe. In 1944, he was flying from London to Paris when his plane disappeared. The plane and Miller were never found.

Swooning Over Sinatra

A young singer named Frank Sinatra had young girls screaming with excitement and fainting in the aisles. Thousands of fans gathered to hear him sing. Thousands more lined the streets hoping to get a glimpse of him or hear a bit of the concert. No other musician had ever created such a stir. His romantic ballads and silky voice drove American women crazy and earned him various nicknames—The King of Swoon, Frank Swoonatra,

The Voice That Thrills Millions, or simply The Voice. Sinatra had battled his way to stardom by singing with big bands. In 1942, he went solo and performed his first of many engagements at the Paramount in New York. Soon,

> "I'm 25. I look maybe 19. Most of the kids feel like I'm one of them—the pal next door, say. So maybe they feel they know me. And that's the way I want it to be."
>
> Frank Sinatra explaining his success with teens

Sinatra was receiving 5,000 fan letters per week. He signed a contract with Columbia Records and agreed to appear in one movie per year. While young people adored him, adults criticized his music and his character. Many of their sons were fighting overseas while Sinatra was earning millions of dollars singing. Still, teens and adults kept buying his records and seeing his movies for decades to come.

■ Big band legend Tommy Dorsey takes the stage with Frank Sinatra.

WORLD FOCUS

CHARLIE PARKER

Many talented musicians were playing jazz music in the 1940s—Kenny Clarke, Tadd Dameron, Thelonius Monk, and Dizzy Gillespie. The man at the top of the list was saxophonist Charlie "Yardbird" Parker. Parker started playing saxophone as a teenager and practiced his art until older musicians took notice. His style was like no one else's—he had the makings of a legend. This new style of jazz called bebop emerged in 1945. Parker and trumpeter Gillespie got together to record the first bebop album. The style took off, and Parker was one of the most influential soloists since Louis Armstrong. Parker and Gillespie recorded several albums together, and by 1955, when Parker died, bebop was the most popular jazz style around.

Allies Meet

In December 1941, President Roosevelt, British Prime Minister Winston Churchill, and their respective advisors gathered in Washington to discuss how they were going to end the war. They agreed that Hitler had to be stopped first, and the battle with Japan would be a U.S. matter. The leaders decided to create a top-level military committee made up of both British and American members. This committee would work in Washington to plan military strategies. Then on January 1, 1942, officials from the U.S., Britain, the Soviet Union, and twenty-three other countries met and agreed to work together to end the war. They would not negotiate separately with the Axis powers. The peace that the Allies promised would be delivered to everyone.

Churchill, Roosevelt, and Stalin met in February 1945. They planned the final attacks

■ Churchill, Roosevelt, and Stalin come together for a historic meeting.

on the Axis powers and discussed Europe's future. In return for Stalin's support in defeating Japan, he was promised several territories, including the return of the Kurile Islands and part of Manchuria, which the Soviet Union had lost to Japan in 1875 and 1904. As well, Churchill and Roosevelt called for democracy in Eastern Europe, a declaration that Stalin ignored.

NATO ESTABLISHED

■ Britain, Luxembourg, France, the Netherlands, and Belgium signed a collective defense agreement in 1948. This alliance needed the military and financial support of the U.S. The North Atlantic Treaty Organization (NATO) talks began immediately, and in 1949, twelve Western countries, including the U.S. and Canada, signed the North Atlantic Treaty. The treaty stated that an attack on one member country would be an attack on all of them. Leaders hoped that, allied in this way, their countries would be able to defend themselves against the growing influence of the Soviet Union. The Soviets were taking over Eastern and Central Europe. U.S. officials called NATO the "antidote to fear," but the establishment of NATO completed the separation of the world into two armed camps.

Worldwide Influence

In 1944, the Soviet Union went from being a victim of Germany to a victor over Germany. Prime Minister Churchill was worried about what would happen once the war was over. He feared that many of the countries would become communist if the Soviet Union had its way. Churchill tried to bring the U.S. on board with his attempt to block Soviet influence.

President Roosevelt was not interested in getting involved. Churchill met with Stalin about how to split up the Balkans region. Churchill wanted to let Stalin control Romania and Bulgaria, while Britain took control of Greece. The two would split Yugoslavia and Hungary fifty-fifty. The deal was never finalized.

President Roosevelt, on the other hand, accepted Soviet expansion. He felt that both countries had interests and they could work them out later. Churchill was disappointed with the lack of alarm in the U.S. Without Roosevelt's military support, Churchill had no other choice than to watch the Soviet army take control of Poland, Romania, Bulgaria, Hungary, and Czechoslovakia.

■ World leaders gather for the first session of the United Nations General Assembly.

Nations Unite

Representatives from the four big powers—the U.S., Britain, the USSR, and China—gathered in Washington, D.C., in 1944. They wanted to find a way to prevent another world war. They worked toward an international organization that would help solve conflicts without war. The four powers wanted to hold most authority, but it soon became obvious that such a system would not work. After six weeks of discussions, the United Nations was created. This organization was to have a general assembly of countries dedicated to peace. There would be a powerful executive council run by the permanent members, which were initially the four powers. Over the next year, details were worked out, and fifty nations came together to promote economic development, world peace, and the protection of human rights.

In 1948, the countries of North and South America met in Colombia to establish the Organization of American States (OAS). This organization promised mutual security for American countries. The OAS was the first regional defense bloc under the United Nations.

Scrambled Names

Unscramble the names of the following 1940s celebrities:

1. S T I N N O W   L I R C H U L C H

2. H I R A C L E   K E P R A R

3. T I A R   T H O R W H A Y

4. F O A L D   L E R I T H

5. C H R I D A L   G R I W T H

Answers:
1. Winston Churchill
2. Charlie Parker
3. Rita Hayworth
4. Adolf Hitler
5. Richard Wright

Multiple Choice

Choose the correct answer from the following multiple choice questions:

1 Franklin D. Roosevelt was the first U.S. president to:
a) die in office.
b) run for, and serve, a third term.
c) meet with Soviet Union officials.

2 Charlie Parker was:
a) in charge of developing atomic weapons for the U.S.
b) a talented jazz musician.
c) charged with tax evasion.

3 Braceros were:
a) agricultural workers, mostly from Mexico.
b) were Italian soldiers fighting in Africa.
c) Air Force heroes.

4 Don Hutson was:
a) the starting pitcher for the New York Yankees.
b) a star wide receiver for the Green Bay Packers.
c) the first African-American judge.

5 The tsunami in Hawai'i:
a) was caused by an earthquake.
b) resulted from the attack on Pearl Harbor.
c) was a military operation.

Answers: 1. b); 2. b); 3. a); 4. b); 5. a).

True or False

1. The Warner Brothers were the first to produce popular animated characters.

2. Mohandas Gandhi was assassinated as he was walking to pray.

3. Only 10,000 Japanese Americans were interned.

4. The war started because of economic sanctions from the West.

5. The United Nations was initiated by the Soviet Union, the United States, Britain, and China.

Answers:
1. False. Disney had already produced popular cartoons.
2. True
3. False. The number was about 110,000.
4. False. The war started when Germany invaded Poland.
5. True

Newsmakers

Match the 1940s newsmakers with their claim to fame.

1. crashed into the Empire State Building

2. Truman's secretary of state

3. wrote a novel about World War II

4. first African American in the major leagues

5. war hero

6. Republican who ran against President Roosevelt

7. Hollywood pin-up

8. pilot who broke the sound barrier

9. composer

10. first American to win Olympic medal in Alpine skiing

d) Jackie Robinson
b) Wendell Willkie
a) Charles Yeager
j) Betty Grable
f) George Marshall
i) Gretchen Fraser
g) Colonel William Smith
e) Norman Mailer
c) Frank Loesser
h) Audie Murphy

Answer: 1. g); 2. f); 3. e); 4. d); 5. h); 6. b); 7. j); 8. a); 9. c); 10. i).

Axis powers: allied countries fighting together, made up of Germany, Italy, and Japan

ballistic: relating to the movements of objects propelled through the air

biblical: of the Bible

conscription: a law making people serve in the military

D-Day: June 6, 1944, the day on which the Allies invaded France to free Europe from the Nazi occupation

demobilized: disbanded after war

discrimination: treating people differently depending on their race

earthenware: pottery made of coarse clay

enlisted: a member of the Armed Forces

escalated: rose, increased

etiquette: the rules of behavior in society

exposés: secrets revealed

fasting: going without food

GI: a member of the U.S. armed forces

grueling: exhausting

internment: confinement

invincible: incapable of being conquered

lynching: killing someone illegally (usually by hanging)

Mach: the ratio of the speed of a body to the speed of sound; Mach 1 is the speed of sound, and Mach 2 is twice the speed of sound

morale: a person's or group's spirit and confidence

radiation: particles emitted by radioactive substances that cause sickness or death

rural electrification: providing homes and businesses in the countryside with electricity

seismograph: an instrument that detects, records, and measures earthquakes

spike: slide into a base with cleats up in an attempt to injure the baseplayer

tribunals: courts of justice

tsunami: a large ocean wave caused by an earthquake

tuberculosis: an infectious disease usually affecting the lungs

vetoed: rejected

Here are some book resources and Internet links if you want to learn more about the people, places, and events that made headlines during the 1940s.

Books

Berlage, Gai. *Women in Baseball*. Westport, CT: Praeger, 1994.

Brewster, Todd and Peter Jennings. *The Century for Young People*. New York: Random House, 1999.

Estrin, Jack C. *American History Made Simple*. New York: The Stonesong Press, 1991.

Rampersad, Arnold. *Jackie Robinson*. New York: Knopf, 1997.

Internet Links

http://www.intelligentsianetwork.com/hollywood-1940s/hollywood-1940s.htm

http://www.mediahistory.com/time/1940s.htm

http://dewey.chs.chico.k12.ca.us/decs4.html

http://www.folksonline.com/folks/hh/tours/1999/forties.htm

For information about other American subjects, type your keywords into a search engine such as Alta Vista or Yahoo!

1940s Index